Remembranc

Remembrance of Crimes Past

Poems 1986–1989

DANNIE ABSE

Hutchinson

London Sydney Auckland Johannesburg

This edition first published in 1990 by
Hutchinson

Century Hutchinson Ltd,
20 Vauxhall Bridge Road, London SW1V 2SA

Century Hutchinson Australia (Pty) Ltd
20 Alfred Street, Milsons Point, Sydney NSW 2061

Century Hutchinson New Zealand Limited
PO Box 40–086, Glenfield, Auckland 10, New Zealand

Century Hutchinson South Africa (Pty) Ltd
PO Box 337, Bergvlei, 2012 South Africa

British Library Cataloguing in Publication Data
Abse, Dannie *1923–*
    Remembrance of crimes past.
    I. Title
    821.914

    ISBN 0–09–174316–8

Phototypeset in Linotron Times
by Input Typesetting Ltd, London
Printed and bound in Great Britain by
Cox and Wyman Ltd.

The right of Dannie Abse to be identified as the
author of this work has been asserted by him
in accordance with the Copyright, Designs
and Patents Act 1988

Acknowledgements

These poems were all written since the publication of *Ask the Bloody Horse*, Hutchinson, London, 1986.

Acknowledgements are owed to the editors of the following magazines where some of these poems had an initial airing: *Acumen*, *Antaeus*, *Encounter*, *Fiction Magazine*, *First and Always* (Faber), *The Georgia Review*, *The Jewish Chronicle*, *The Listener*, *New Poetry 2* (PEN), *The New Welsh Review*, *The Observer*, *The Poetry Book Society Anthology* 1986–87 and 1987–88, *Poetry (Chicago)*, *Poetry Review*, *Poetry Wales*, *Prospice 25*, *Thames Poetry*, and *Time for Verse* (BBC).

Some of the poems appeared in *Sky in Narrow Streets*, Quarterly Review of Literature Poetry Series VIII, Princeton, USA, 1987.

One poem, 'Carnal Knowledge', was included in *White Coat, Purple Coat*, Hutchinson, London, 1989.

Contents

A Wall

in a field in the County of Glamorgan.
You won't find it named in any guidebook.
It lies, plonk, in the middle of rising ground,
forty-four paces long, high as your eyes,
it begins for no reason, ends no place.
No other walls are adjacent to it.
Seemingly unremarkable, it's just there,
stones of different sizes, different greys.

Don't say this wall is useless, that the grass
on the shadow side is much like the other.
It exists for golden lichens to settle,
for butterflies in their obstacle race
chasing each other to the winning post,
for huddling sheep in a slanting rainfall,
for you to say, 'This wall is beautiful.'

Dulciana

Waking this morning
I feel uneasy,
as if there were important words
I had forgotten to utter,
like letters unanswered,
like invitations neglected.

Asleep, everyone's enslaved
and, at dawn, when most
are blindfolded,
the Firing Squad
takes up its position.

Now, though, I'm wide awake
and still feel accused
by secret words
from another century.

Yes, to abuse words
is to smear blood on a silken garment;
and yes, there are so many
so many words in the dictionary
I have never used –
some undiscovered,
some half-remembered or half-heard,
like the distant, honeyless
buzz of prayer.

So many English words

I have no knowledge of –
less like places never visited
than like places never imagined.
Or like those numberless doors
I never forced back
to disclose the life I've never led.

Downstairs, impelled,
I open the dictionary
at random
and let my index finger fall
where it will.

I read: DULCIANA
'an 8-foot organ stop
of a soft string-like tone'.

The Lesson of Han Fei

'I'm committed,' I gabbled
(in my dream) to the ghost
the colour of water
shaking like water disturbed.
'Committed to difficulty.'
This was in Peking, I think,
a city I have never visited.
He introduced himself
shyly, as Han Fei,
painter-philosopher
of the third century BC.
We discussed, of course,
the water in watercolours
and the art of Art,
he of the legalist school,
and I, like a fool,
consulting a Chinese-
English phrase book.

This morning, nothing else
of our sweet debate recalled
except his valediction:
'It's hard, sir, hard, hard
to paint a horse or a dog
but easy, damnably easy
to paint a ghost.'
Then bowing gracefully low
he deleted himself,
not even leaving

the smell of a watermark;
and I journeyed on
above an epidemic of ghosts
(shouts from the abyss)
to the Twentieth Century,
my eyes opening to
the water on the windowpane
of a familiar bedroom.

That was hardly an hour ago,
and now, tea-sober, I add,
for the sake of prosaic truth,
(it is still raining)
never have I written a poem
with such damnable ease as this,
'The Lesson of Han Fei'.

Logocracy

The lion hugely roared. 'What? What?'
The barbarians cataleptic, open-mouthed.
Never had they heard one like,
never had they seen one such.

This too-strange obstacle to Rome,
this testicled adversary unknown.
They parleyed, would not march on.
An omen? A stern god, disguised?

Their leader, word-acrobat
and soul-physician, lied soothingly.
'Only a Roman dog,' he smiled.
'What an amusing bark,' he cried.

So, becalmed, the barbarians
with enthusiastic clubs
beat and beat that manic dog
till its stentorian roaring died.

Of Itzig and the Horse

Now, at dusk, through these binoculars
little Itzig still unsteady
on the galloping animal –
his arms about the horse's neck,
his head behind the horse's head.

And still that bandy fool is talking.
How weirdly innocent he is.
He doesn't know that he is bugged,
that we hear him mutter pleas to God.
Or is he talking to the horse?

The Professor then astounds us.
'That speech, gentlemen, is inhuman.
First, focus your binoculars.
Is it Itzig's mouth that's moving
or is the horse's mouth agape?

'Those hoarse soundings are a horse's,
those fine contractions of the glottis
are indubitably equine:
the expiration before the media
as well as before the tenuis.

'Yes it's odd, dear sirs, quite odd,
but is that horse addressing Itzig
or does the horse converse with God?'
We observe the moon above the hill
and the rider going under it.

7

The Origin of Music

When I was a medical student
I stole two femurs of a baby
from The Pathology Specimen Room.
Now I keep them in my pocket,
the right femur and the left femur.
Like a boy scout, I'm prepared.
For what can one say to a neighbour
when his wife dies? 'Sorry'?
Or when a friend's sweet child
suffers leukaemia? 'Condolences'?
No, if I should meet either friend
or stricken neighbour in the street
and he should tell me, whisper to me,
his woeful, intimate news,
wordless I take the two small femurs
from out of my pocket sadly
and play them like castanets.

Anti-Clockwise (1)

'Nothing to do with sex, doctor.' Her voice dies.
In the consulting room's firegrate, no fire.
Last summer's dried flowers, sweet lies, nest there.

Now if through her eyes I could slowly pan,
with ophthalmoscope, would I blunderingly
light up single beds in separate bedrooms?

Whispers and sighs. I cannot say, 'What?' again.
So observe her mouth's theatre, how she turns
and turns her wedding ring, anti-clockwise.

Anti-Clockwise (2)

Before breakfast, from my bedroom window,
behold jogging Des, our grey-haired neighbour,
conspicuous in vest and shorts – how he
puffs and blows past our railings.
Rejuvenation therapy, he says.

I think of Abishag the Shunammite,
that most beautiful girl – sheer dynamite –
she ministered to the aged King.
Disaster: he knew her not. Soon was dead.
And Hermann Boerhaave, that Dutch physician,

(13th century) sweet buttery girls failing,
thought he would undo the mortal lock
by placing, instead, two untrousered youths
each side of the prostrate burgomaster.
With what results nobody knows. Don't mock,

only the young don't wish to be younger.
Some, credulous, still receive intramuscular
drug-muck, testicular extracts; some just
eat yoghurt. Once some blithely feasted
on viper-meat or drank youthful blood (cheers!)

from freshly opened veins – and not always
volunteers. So I suppose it's better
that my cock and cardiac-minded neighbour
this bright and bloody early morning
(his doleful wife still staring at the ceiling)

should run anti-clockwise round the block.

Carnal Knowledge

1

You, student, whistling those elusive bits
of Schubert when phut, phut, phut, throbbed the sky
of London. Listen: the servo-engine cut
and the silence was not the desired silence
between two movements of music. Then
Finale, the Aldwych echo of crunch
and the urgent ambulances loaded
with the fresh dead. You, young, whistled again,
entered King's, climbed the stone-murky steps
to the high and brilliant Dissecting Room
where nameless others, naked on the slabs,
reclined in disgraceful silences – twenty
amazing sculptures waiting to be vandalized.

2

You, corpse, I pried into your bloodless meat
without the morbid curiosity of Vesalius,
did not care that the great Galen was wrong,
Avicenna mistaken, that they had described
the approximate structure of pigs and monkeys
rather than the human body. With scalpel
I dug deep into your stale formaldehyde
unaware of Pope Boniface's decree
but, as instructed, violated you –
the reek of you in my eyes, my nostrils,
clothes, in the kisses of my girlfriends.
You, anonymous. Who were you, mister?

Your thin mouth could not reply, 'Absent, sir,'
or utter with inquisitionary rage.

Your neck exposed, muscles, nerves, vessels,
a mere coloured plate in some anatomy book;
your right hand, too, dissected, never belonged,
it seemed, to somebody once shockingly alive,
never held, surely, another hand in greeting
or tenderness, never clenched a fist in anger,
never took up a pen to sign an authentic name.

You, dead man, Thing, each day, each week,
each month, you, slowly decreasing Thing,
visibly losing Divine proportions,
you residue, mere trunk of a man's body,
you, X, legless, armless, headless Thing
that I dissected so casually.

Then went downstairs to drink wartime coffee.

3
When the hospital priest, Father Jerome,
remarked, 'The Devil made the lower parts
of a man's body, God the upper,'
I said, 'Father, it's the other way round.'
So, the anatomy course over, Jerome,
thanatologist, did not invite me
to the Special Service for the Twenty Dead,
did not say to me, 'Come for the relatives' sake.'
(Surprise, surprise, that they had relatives,
those lifeless-size, innominate creatures.)

Other students accepted, joined in the fake chanting,
organ solemnity, cobwebbed theatre.
And that's all it would have been,
a ceremony propitious and routine,
an obligation forgotten soon enough
had not the strict priest with premeditated rage
called out the Register of the Twenty Dead –

each non-cephalic carcass gloatingly identified
with a local habitation and a name
till one by one, made culpable, the students cried.

4
I did not learn the name of my intimate,
the twentieth sculpture, the one next to the door.
No matter. Now all these years later
I know those twenty sculptures were but one,
the same one duplicated. You.
I hear not Father Jerome but St Jerome cry,
'No, John will be John, Mary will be Mary,'
as if the dead would have ears to hear
the Register on Judgement Day.
    Look, on gravestones many names.
There should be one only. Yours.
No, not even one since you have no name.
In the newspapers' memorial columns
many names. A joke.
On the canvases of masterpieces
the same figure always in disguise. Yours.
Even in the portraits of the old anchorite
fingering a dry skull you are half concealed
lest onlookers should turn away blinded.
In certain music, too, with its sound of loss,
in that Schubert Quintet, for instance,
you are there in the Adagio,
playing the third cello that cannot be heard.
    You are there and there and there, nameless,
and here I am, older by far and nearer,
perplexed, trying to recall what you looked like
before I dissected your face – you, threat,
molesting presence, and I in a white coat
your enemy, in a purple one, your nuncio,
writing this while a winter twig, not you,
scrapes, scrapes the windowpane.

Soon I shall climb the stairs. Gratefully,
I shall wind up the usual clock at bedtime
(the steam vanishing from the bathroom mirror)
with my hand, my living hand.

A Prescription

Sweet-tempered, pestering
young man of Oxford
juggling with ghazals,
tercets, haikus, tankas,
not to mention villanelles,
terzanelles and rondelets;
conversant with the phonetic
kinships of rhyme, assonance
and consonance; the four
nuances of stress, the three
junctions; forget now
the skeltonic couplet,
the heroic couplet, the split
couplet, the poulter's measure;
speak not of englyn
penfyr, englyn milwr;
but westward hasten
to that rising, lonely ground
between the evening rivers,
the alder-gazing rivers,
Mawddach and Dysynni.

Let it be dark when, alone,
you climb the awful mountain
so that you can count the stars.
Ignore the giant shufflings
behind you – put out that torch! –
the far intermittent cries
of the nocturnal birds

– if birds they are –
their small screams of torture.
Instead, scholar as you are,
remark the old proverb
how the one who ascends
Cadair Idris at night
comes back in dawn's light
lately mad or a great poet.
Meanwhile, I'll wait here
in this dull room of urine-
flask, weighing-machine,
examination-couch, X-ray screen,
for your return (triumphant
or bizarre) patiently.

Arianrhod

Not Arianrhod of Swansea
who could have become a nun,
not cold-flame Arianrhod?
Once, near poppydrowsing corn,
through the cricket weather
consentiently together;
but twice the quarrels after,
dissonances and disorder,
eye-bright denunciations
from theological Arianrhod,
disinclined Arianrhod,
while two rivers were meeting
at Pontneathvaughan.

Night-war came to Swansea
when the kettle was whistling,
Bowdler lay deeper
in Mumbles' graveyard.
Hurdling fire turned to fire
the things it first charred –
both gone Arianrhod's parents
who wailed with the siren,
that ghost-factory siren;
and later stunned Arianrhod
diminished in hospital,
tongue-rotted in hospital,
because their going was hard.

Do names have destinies?
Today in a chronic ward
another Arianrhod, a schizophrene,
picking the frost from her face.
Then back down the landing
heard myself mumbling – Destiny
itself is a man-made name.
Out through the front gate
but still see her standing
on light-iced linoleum,
that used one, Arianrhod,
figure a matchstick,
flame gone without trace.

A Conspicuous Couple

'You and you are sure together
As the winter to foul weather' – As You Like It

Bubbles, brass, gaudy things, they loved well,
all that glitters and is starred,
the seven fairground colours swanking
on the bevelled edge of glass –
she, dramatic as a sunset,
he, chromatic like a rainbow
or an oilpool in the yard.

Love, agog, italic, rang their bell:
her computer flashing like a million,
he, randy, sighing like a villain;
she spread, he swooped, a kingfisher,
a kind of flying oilpool –
how they fluttered, how they fired,
till they guttered on her bed.

Naughty Aphrodite (minus nightie)
surely blessed them when they married,
outstaining the stained church window;
not the spermless priest who muttered,
'With this paintbox I thee wed,
a sunset to a rainbow
or an aurora borealis.'

The best man's innuendos –
he was importune and loaded;

19

the aunts goofy and embarrassed
for no kiss could be more sexy
to erect in church a boudoir.
And big the triumph of the organ
when, promptly, the choirboys exploded.

Advice to Married Women

Beautiful married women
of the world,
reflect on the story
of Lady Caroline Lamb
who hopped around the room
because the parrot
bit her big toe;

remember Byron's rage,
how he, her lover,
somewhat macho,
picked up the creature;
how, when he hurled it
across the room,
the bird screamed out,
'Johnny!'

So consider which pets
you should keep:
dogs OK,
cats OK
and, of course, those dumb
goldfish constantly
chewing gum –
no problem.

But parrots?
Verboten,
gwaharddedig,

interdit,
prohibido,
vietato,
zakázano.

Heed what I say
beautiful married women
of the world
lest you too be hurled
across a thousand rooms
and your sweet, pink,
wet tongues
be cut out, verily.

The Wife of Columbus

After I made love
to the wife of Christopher Columbus
I woke up. Later, over breakfast,
I consulted a map.
Had I not kissed a birthmark
on the soft inside of her right thigh,
a birthmark that resembled
the contours of an island,
familiar but forgotten?
And yet, not necessarily an island.
Error? Columbus thought he'd reached
the spice-rich coast of India.

I have visited, in real daylight,
Columbus, capital of Ohio,
observed Doric buildings
under island-clouds. I have walked
past the Institute of the Blind
questing for something lost, once seen;
also past the Penitentiary
and the Catholic Cathedral
where tall and short women entered,
some hiding their faces
as she did once when the three ships
set sail from the quay at Palos.

Error. I should have journeyed
to a place not on my itinerary –
Columbus, Georgia, perhaps,

and walked all the moody afternoon
beside the Chattahoochee river
searching for a sign;
or Columbus, Indiana, say,
and waited like one asleep
at its junction of railways
for a train of many windows –
with so many sitting skeletons,
so many skulls staring out.

The Ocnophil and the Philobat

Distant the city lights. Now at nightfall
I imagine writ above this ruined door
that opens to a blackness which descends:
'Visitor, discover Nothing here. Endure'.
I dreamed that once and still the words pursue.
I wouldn't go down there if I were you.

I had another dream the other night:
slopes of snow; standing figures cut from ice,
shaped like Henry Moores. They seemed to threaten,
they dragged behind them, blurred and imprecise,
shadows owning a red or purplish hue.
I wouldn't go down there if I were you.

Stone balustrades wind round into the dark
and I drop a stone. So long before it lands.
You remark, 'I'd like to see what lies below,'
and nonchalantly offer me your hand
although the roof above is all askew.
I wouldn't go down there if I . . . *Careful!*

Still you insist and beckon me to come
and childlike shout, 'I dare you. Take a chance,
the more we experience the more we know
and the more we journey into ignorance.'
Agreed, but there are doors I'll not go through.
I wouldn't go down there if I were you.

Musical Moments

1. His Last Piano Lesson (1933)
    'Poet, be seated at the piano.' – Wallace Stevens

When, after tea,
(Germany still six million
miles away) Miss Crouch,
the upright piano teacher,
knocks at the front door
the boy's at the back door.
Numbly bored with scales
nimbly scales the wall

and hearing in the park
the pointless cries of children,
joins butter-fingered Jack
and his high-flung tennis ball.

There backslangs
and jabberwocks
swaps acid-drops for bull's-eyes,
Hammond for Hobbs,
and one pocket-aged
PK chewing gum –

till the park-keeper comes
stamping the gravel path,
blowing his whistle,
making the sparrows fly
from their scattered park bench crumbs

(their little noise
the shaking of umbrellas).

Back home, downstairs,
the piano-lid's closed,
a coffin of music.
Their war-faces, their big thumbs.

Exiguous memory:
Remembrance of Crimes Past, 1933,
so few and so many!
On the sideboard,
walnuts in a cut-glass bowl,
and the father raging,
'That's his last piano lesson.'

O joy, Miss dismissed!

Later, only the landing light
under the bedroom door:
no hectoring voices,
no blameless man-sized scarecrow
being thumped down the carpeted stairs
with sovereign impunity

before Sleep's grisly fictions
and forgeries of the world.

2. Outside a Graveyard (1989)
    *'One day, the piano has all the colours of the orchestra;
    another day, it brings forth sounds that come from other
    worlds.'* – Edwin Fischer

Many nearer than you have gone, too many,
so your going does not touch me deeply,

a one-fingered piano note only
soft as a caress, sounding regret
and then again regret, diminuendo,
spare – hardly a Wagnerian Funeral March;
yet I want to say, 'Sorry, Miss Crouch,'
now that you are dismissed forever.
You were so unassuming and gentle.
If there's a heaven, that's your address.

Once, after the war, I observed you
at a romantic Moiseiwitsch concert,
at Cardiff's plush Empire (so soon after
demolished, replaced by a neon-lit superstore).
You sat thrilled in the stalls, eyes raptly shut
– not in the insanity of prayer but
as if that music was making love to you.

Now I stare at church gargoyles, church spire,
then close my eyes also. Wait! Be patient! Look!
The Assumption of Miss Crouch. There! Up there!
Several hundred feet above the spire,
blessed and sedate in evening dress,
rising slowly above Glamorganshire,
you, old lady, playing the piano –
not an upright piece of furniture either
but a concert-hall, exalted Bechstein,
its one black wing uplifted and beating,
bringing forth sounds from another world,
yes, you and the piano triumphantly rising
between the clouds, higher and higher.

In Jerusalem

Like walking through a perfume factory
with attar of rose, macerated violet,
oil of jasmine, censored by a heavy cold.

Or far from home, the language double-Dutch,
the room a riot of open mouths. 'What? What?'
All laughing at a joke except yourself.

That aurulent Fall in Washington, remember,
at the National Gallery? A blind girl
with her blond fiancé facing a Monet.

Outside Vienna, they said to Beethoven,
'Charming, don't you agree, those distant cowbells?'
Suddenly, he wept. They thought, 'These musicians.'

Thirty years ago, in the ward, the hunchback
with syringomyelia. He could not feel
the lit cigarette smouldering his forearm.

Now here I am, motionless as a question mark,
while each bearded man in tasselled shawl
hums and sways. The exclusivity of prayer!

If it is a prayer and not an orgy where
all – such busy cries and torment – fornicate
with holy spirits against a wall.

A Footnote Extended

for Thomas Szasz's *Karl Kraus and the Soul Doctors*

Dr Szasz, professor, sir,
I read your book.
I won't make criticisms (I could)
but more attention, please,
for Egon Friedman,
born in Vienna, 1878,
of Jewish parents.

Who, insulted, endured.
Who studied in Berlin,
later in Heidelberg:
studied German
studied philosophy
studied natural science;
did not write a treatise
on the whale,
that hunted mammal
posing as a fish.

But returned to Vienna,
changed his visiting card.
Friedell now, not Friedman.
'Hello Dr Friedell,
you're a mensch, Dr Friedell.
Here's a bowl of wax apples,
here's a vase of paper flowers,
here's margarine in a lordly dish.'

He ignored such tauntings.
Tall, he turned the other cheek,
he converted to Christianity –
defended the Gospel
against Mosaic subversion;
attacked the Jewish Science
of Psychoanalysis,
called its practitioners –
Freud, Abraham, Stekel –
'underground blood-suckers'.

Ah, applause now
for the proselyte
so soon to be successful,
so edgily celebrated
under the probing, chalky
spotlight of cabaret-actor,
writer, critic, author of
Cultural History of the Modern Age.

When the Nazis marched
into Austria
– strange amphigouri
of circumstance –
Friedell, in his bachelor room,
walked towards the long mirror,
saw Friedman approaching.
Whispered Friedman,
screamed FRIEDMAN,
and killed himself.

Of Two Languages

(for Hanoch Bartov)

1

Citizen Dov walking on Mount Carmel
heard Agnon speaking Yiddish to a companion.
'How can you,' complained Dov, 'a five-star scholar,
a great *Hebrew* author, a Nobel prize winner,
prophet amongst men, Solomon amongst Kings,
a genuine, first-class somebody (destined for
a state funeral) how can *you* speak Yiddish?'

'Observe which way we're walking,' replied Agnon.
'Downhill. Downhill, I always speak Yiddish.
Uphill – break forth into singing, ye mountains –
uphill, I speak the language of Isaiah.'

2

Dov, you know Hebrew, you also know Yiddish.
Did you not speak to God in Hebrew
when you spoke to men in Yiddish?

All those used-up, ascetic centuries
of studying the evidence of 22 consonants;
the 23rd would not have destroyed the world.

Now in Hebrew, bellicose, you say, 'Go away.'
Once, softly in Yiddish, you begged, 'Leave me alone.'

Tell me, what's the word for 'mercy' in Hebrew?
In Yiddish, 'mercy' must have many synonyms.

Say now in Yiddish:
'Exile. Pogrom. Wandering. Holocaust.'
Say now in Hebrew:
'Blessed Art Thou O Lord.'

White Balloon

Dear love, Auschwitz made me
more of a Jew than ever Moses did.
But the world's not always with us.
Happiness enters here again tonight
like an unexpected guest
with no memory of the future either;

enters with such an italic emphasis,
jubilant, announcing triumphantly
hey presto and here I am and opening
the June door into our night living room
where under the lampshade's ciliate
an armchair's occupied by a white balloon.
As if there'd been a party.

Of course, Happiness, uninhibited,
will pick it up, his stroking thumb
squeaking a little as he leads us to the hall.
And we shall follow him, too,
when he climbs the lit staircase
towards the landing's darkness,
bouncing bouncing the white balloon
from hand to hand.

It's bedtime; soon we must dream
separately – but what does it matter now
as the white balloon is thrown up high?
Quiet, so quiet, the moon above Masada
and closed, abandoned for the night,
the icecream van at Auschwitz.

A Small Farmhouse Near Brno

What could David Molko do,
in that age of local pogroms
when, forlorn, they appeared in his yard,
those bearded cousins, their wives and children,
who had been fed only on saliva,
the tall and pale and the small and pale,
tearful, destitute, distraught?

'My home's your home,' said Molko,
'the air I breathe will be the air
you breathe. As Ben Azzai promised,
you'll be called by your name,
you'll be given what is yours,
you'll be seated in your place.'

And that first night, near or at the table,
they all sang solemnly, even the children,
to the mournful tune of the Hatikvah:
'Austria, Rumania and Russia too,
all combine to persecute the Jew.'
Then all sat to eat of Molko's meat,
then all stood to drink from Molko's cup.

But it came to pass, nights moonlit or moonless,
they did not sing. Instead, discordances,
small quarrels, nags, weepings, sulks,
gnashing of teeth. For fifteen heads slept
in a farmhouse meant for three or four
and even Molko's equable wife

loudly whispered, 'In the belly
of the fish, Jonah, afflicted,
had more room than we have here.'

Molko, being Molko, consulted the rabbi,
the very old, quivering rabbi,
wise as Shammai, as Hillel even.
He said,
          'Behold, you have chickens, Molko,
white chickens and brown chickens,
in the yard you have chickens.
Therefore I say unto you, Molko,
take them into the house also,
the white and the brown chickens,
those that lay white eggs and
those that lay brown eggs.'

Molko, dubiously, took in the chickens.
And it was worse. Only three nights later
he woke from a nightmare shouting,
'More air, more air.' So, at the hour
when great kings set forth to battle,
Molko once more came unto that rabbi
wise as Shammai, as Hillel even,
who said,
            'Behold, you have four goats, Molko.
I have seen them in your yard.
Though not writ in the chronicles
of the kings of Israel I say unto you
take them in, take the four goats in also.'

Molko stared at the palms of his hands.
But the rabbi told how things bitter
can be made sweet, how the lupine
when diligently boiled, soaked seven times

in water, is made so – as mustard is
or the astringent caper-plant.

So Molko took in the goats,
even the very smelly one he called Buz, the son
of the billy goat Guzi, the son of Toah,
the son of Zuph, the son of Asaph.
And it was worse.

'O Lord hear,' cried Molko's agitated wife
and 'O Lord forgive,' and 'O Lord
hearken and do.' So that after three sabbaths
Molko came once more unto the rabbi
who said,
             'Behold, you have no oxen, Molko,
you have no mules, but you own a donkey.
How manifold are Thy works, O Lord.
Yes, take the donkey who trembles like I do
into your sanctuary. As the Lord liveth,
and as I have two changes of garments,
all will be well, trust me, believe me.'

Thus Molko took into his farmhouse
the donkey that stared at the stinking goats,
that stared at the twelve feathered fowl,
the brown ones and the white ones.
And it was worse.

All fifteen in the little house,
the bearded ones and the unbearded ones,
screamed that it was worse, it was much worse –
like after the desolation of Sodom
and, possibly, Gomorrah.

Now Molko came unto the rabbi
crying, 'Woe, woe,' and his right eye runneth

with water and his left eye runneth
with water. So the rabbi pondered
who had studied all the sages of Israel
and said,
      'Behold, I shall deliver thee.
Take out the donkey, yes, take it out
though like me the donkey feels cold
even in June.'

Molko took the donkey out
into the yard, the uncomprehending donkey.
And it was better. But still
the house quarrelled, gnashed its teeth.
So the rabbi stood on one leg
like Hillel, swaying, vibrating,
till wondrously inspired
he said,
      'Behold, take out the four goats
especially Buz, the son
of the billy goat Guzi, the son of Toah,
the son of Zuph, the son of Asaph.'
And lo, Molko obeyed.
And it was better.

But still the house lacked oxygen:
the crying of the children,
the shouting of the women,
the cursing of the bearded ones,
so the rabbi, the very old and wise rabbi
called out,
      'Behold, take out the chickens,
take out the brown ones and the white ones –'
and lo, when the fowl were back in the yard
it was better, oh yes it was better,
and everybody was happy,
so that all now cried out,

'Blessed be the Lord for we are rich,'
and suddenly, it seemed, the little farmhouse
had the height of cedars.
Then they sang near or at the table,
'Austria, Rumania and Russia too,
all combine to persecute the Jew.'

Smiling Through

'All great art is praise' – John Ruskin

1

Then there's the parable of three wise men
(always three, as in a joke) who walk
in their fresh linen through the sweet morning
till they hear fat busy flies, see a dog,
stiff legs in the air, disintegrating.
'What a terrible sight!' cries the first beard.
'What a terrible smell!' complains the second.
'What lovely white teeth,' the third, rapturously.

2

The scandalous paradox of cripples
and slums in a world of colours.

Praise the white tooth?

The expensive bombs blessed with holy cries
falling on the screams of mothers.

Praise the white tooth.

3

Meanwhile, sky in narrow streets;
yet turning the hands of a clock,
as one might do at bedtime
(though it is only afternoon)
something may fall away or arrive:

another place, a beautiful
virus-free clearing where, of course,
everybody is so happy –
not least the three up-market shepherds –
everything grassy and bird song,
flower-pretty and river sound,
the sky blue blue blue everywhere
over this landscape waiting for
a Poussin. But look – in the dark
green shadow of that light green tree
a human skull, teeth in its jaw
uttering, 'I, too, am in Arcady.'

4
The famine babies with ponderous eyes
in a careless world of plenty.

Praise the white tooth?

The future with Chernobyl disease
in one year or in twenty?

Praise the white tooth.
Praise the white tooth.

Dog on a Rubbish Tip

This cowering, apocalyptic sky,
light not to be believed,
of impending thunder
and the dark, granular tip
of rubble, charred pulp, tyres
where, improbably, an ancestor
of the totems,
retaining the faculty
of metamorphosis,
chooses the shape of a dog.

Tip, like modern outdoor sculpture,
where a dog hirples for a bone.
The scent teases magnetically,
back and fore, the lodestone-
heavy nose of the dog.
Surprise: has the dog discovered
the bone of a dog?
The wind must have whistled it
to this dishabited
outpost, city's detritus.

The dog, now, master and scholar,
knows that the bone, if bone,
is feigning death. This angers him.
In the dog's grinning mouth
the bone undergoes a seizure.
It cannot resist
its assailant. Its spirit

weeps. In a mania of
paroxysm the dog, exorcist,
shakes it and shakes it.

Ovid should tell this story
of a dog on a rubbish tip.
The sky crackles elsewhere,
the bone is paying its debt
till, at last, dropped, ignored.
Once more dog becomes slave
to the zigzag electric scent
active under the rubble.
Black nose pulled back and fore,
bone changing into a stick.

Magnolia, Golders Hill Park (1)

In the park's walled garden,
beneath the candelabra
of a magnolia tree,
I know a grained wooden seat
that those in distress
should sit upon in silence
when the tree's tonic flowering
is more holy than
a cathedral;
but let no virgin dare
to sit there after dark
lest next morning, profaned,
she be found loitering,
shouting unrestrained, 'Rape! Rape!',
dazed, shivering and insane,
with the tree's white blossom
wildly scattered on the ground,
a little blood-stained.

Magnolia, Golders Hill Park (2)

Now in a dusty July
that will not come again,
I come again to this walled garden
past wooden seats inscribed:
IN MEMORY OF JANE FREEMAN,
IN MEMORY OF DORIS ABBOTS,
IN LOVING MEMORY
OF JOHN CONNELL RIP,
IN FONDEST MEMORY
OF SYLVIA LENNARD
WHO LOVED LIFE,
IN REMEMBRANCE
OF DAVID PERKINS
WHO LOVED THIS GARDEN,
IN LOVING MEMORY
OF DAD, ARTHUR ADAMS,
until I feel myself to be
the word DESOLATION,
wasting the afternoon away,
scribbling these pencilled lines
beneath a magnolia tree
now, itself, so humdrum a green,
so inconspicuous – like Pierre Magnol,
French botanist of the 17th century,
unknown today, his life wiped clean,
except he named this genus of tree:
the magnolia soulangeana,

the umbrella, the sweet bay,
the magnolia grandiflora
or bull bay,
and yulan, the Chinese magnolia.

Ancestor

Black-bearded, white-toothed, lantern-jawed
Antara al-Abse of the sixth century,
remote desert prince, poet of battles,
who answered to no one 'Sir' or 'Lord';
fabulous Bedouin, Maverick and Strong-man,
of white father and black mother, who wrote,
'Half of me comes from the family of Abse,
the other half I defend with my sword.'

I see you approaching the blood-spitting crowd
that backed away from an enormous bull.
'Only Antara can fight this one,' they cried.
If, now, I claim you as my ancestor,
it's not because of your name or fame;
it's because you so temperately sighed,
'Ah yes. But does that bull know I'm Antara?'
And turned away knowing the value of pride.

Staring at a Chandelier

True ancestors of mine,
those in hell, those in heaven,
they're not big wheels
like roaring, war-loving Antara.
They've been allocated
only small, menial jobs,
nothing extraordinary.

In hell,
they're working in the boiler-rooms,
fags scuttling for the great stokers
(dry in the air, plain H_2S);
in hell they're tea-boys for the damned
cigar-smoking disc jockeys
who play otitis media pop music.

In heaven
they're mere storekeepers for the harps
(subtle perfumes of jasmine and ambergris);
in heaven they're brushing down
angel wings or polishing the haloes
– the standard, economy type,
not the real, business-class, gold ones.

How do I know all this,
I, inappropriately dressed
in my one and only suit
(now visibly fatigued, tight-fitting)
kept for formal occasions,

for functions and funerals
of the last twenty-five years?

I had the sense of it in the queue
when the six-foot-four flunkey
shouted, 'Her Highness, the Duchess of This,'
and 'Air Vice-Marshal What,'
and 'General Hyphenated-Why,'
and 'Lord and Lady That,'
then asked me, three times, to repeat my name.

Soon after, I saw it in the predictable
dazzle of a chandelier
high above those ageing folk
gathering in gowns and uniforms
on the red carpet under it
and who, when next I looked,
like the tall flunkey, had vanished.

At Ogmore-by-Sea This August Evening

I think of one who loved this estuary –
my father – who, self-taught, scraped upon
an obstinate violin. Now, in a room
darker than the darkening evening outside,
I choose a solemn record, listen to
a violinist inhabit a Bach partita.
This violinist and violin are unified.

Such power! The music summons night. What more?
It's twenty minutes later into August
before the gaudy sun sinks to Australia.
Now nearer than the promontory paw
and wincing electric of Porthcawl
look! the death-boat black as anthracite,
at its spotlit prow a pale familiar.

Father? Here I am, Father. I see you
jubilantly lit, an ordered carnival.
The tide's in. From Nash Point no foghorns howl.
I'm at your favourite place where once you held
a bending rod and taught me how to bait
the ragworm hooks. Here, Father, here, tonight
we'll catch a bass or two, or dabs, or cod.

Senseless conjuration! I wipe my smile away
for now, lit at the prow, not my father
but his skeleton stands. The spotlight fails,

the occult boat's a smudge while three far lighthouses
converse in dotty exclamation marks.
The ciaccona's over, the record played,
there's nothing but the tumult of the sea.

Brueghel in Naples

'About suffering they were never wrong,
The Old Masters . . .' – W H Auden

Ovid would never have guessed how far
and Father's notion about wax melting, bah!
It's ice up there. Freezing.
Soaring and swooping over solitary altitudes
I was breezing along (a record I should think)
when my wings began to moult not melt.
These days, workmanship, I ask you.
Appalling.

There's a mountain down there on fire
and I'm falling, falling away from it.
Phew, the sun's on the horizon
or am I upside down?

Great Bacchus, the sea is rearing
up. Will I drown? My white legs
the last to disappear? (I have no trousers on.)
A little to the left the ploughman,
a little to the right a galleon,
a sailor climbing the rigging,
a fisherman casting his line,
and now I hear a shepherd's dog barking.
I'm that near.

Lest I leave no trace
but a few scattered feathers on the water

show me your face, sailor,
look up, fisherman,
look this way, shepherd,
turn around, ploughman.
Raise the alarm! Launch a boat!

My luck. I'm seen
only by a jackass of an artist
interested in composition, in the green
tinge of the sea, in the aesthetics
of disaster – not in me.

I drown, bubble by bubble,
(Help! Save me!)
while he stands ruthlessly
before the canvas, busy busy,
intent on becoming an Old Master.

Not in Proper Light

'I am there where no news even of myself reaches me.'

In a small room at dawn a grey man sits
(outside the demented birds are praying)
at a table, motionless. The letter
to nobody is finished and signed
'Itzig' who, of course, does not exist.

   'Dear No body,
   before unease and disease,
   before the bacterial flora
   in the human bowel,
   before Eve, before Lilith
   was returned to dust in a sunbeam,
   before Adam, before Adam had
   compassion or reason; before
   the tellurian spirit entered Adam;
   before the golem that was Adam,
   the clouds above.

The sun above the clouds
above the earth beautiful:
the trees the lakes the mountains,
the birds in the trees,
the fish in the lakes,
the animals in the mountains –
everything bountiful,

but no speech.

54

So God in his boredom
created languages.
The birds in the trees
could not understand them,
no creature could cry "Joy" or "Glory",
no one could beg "Please",
no one could sigh "Thank you".
Hence men and women were created

but some cursed.'

Now in the slow dolorous light
(the imaginary lampshade still active)
Itzig, who does not exist, tears up
the letter, tears up what he has torn
then lets float each fragment of paper
that obeying the laws of gravity
reluctantly, so reluctantly,
spirals to the wastepaper basket.

Look, one piece, two pieces, sideways
miss, settle on the carpet.

Except that in proper light
there is no wastepaper basket, no carpet.

The Gates of Paradise

The Baptistery, Florence

Who'd not hesitate before these gilded doors
that Michelangelo, amazed, once described
as gates to grace the entrance to Paradise?

So much we lack, but mere intimate silence
lies within: the coolest shade, the font, the tomb,
and signs, on the marble, of the zodiac.

Besides, sunstruck, the animate street's outside;
so turn these great shut doors around, front to back
that their name, one perfect day, be accurate.